Sweepin Glass

P O E M S

Sweeping Glass
P O E M S

Jody Serey

Copyright © 2024 Jody Serey
All rights reserved. No part of this book may be reproduced in any form or by electronic or mechanical means, including information storage and retrieval systems, without permission in writing from the publisher, except by a reviewer who may quote brief passages in a review.

The events and conversations in this book have been set down to the best of the author's ability, although some names and details have been changed or omitted to protect the privacy of individuals.

Published in the United States by
Serey/Jones Publishers, Inc.
www.sereyjones.com

ISBN: 9781881276340 (paperback)

ABOUT THIS BOOK

The title of this book is *Sweeping Glass*, and reflects a skill passed onto me by my mother.

This collection contains poems that I created over a span of more than 50 years. They appear in alphabetical order just to keep them corralled in some kind of logical order. A few have dates, which refer to when actual events occurred — **not** when a poem was written. All were composed whenever I had the chance. They are raw, uneven in quality, and frank. If you know me, nothing will surprise you.

This book is dedicated to my mother, Betty Mullins Jones, who bought me my first harmonica and taught me to drive a stick shift. I loved her more than she ever suspected.

Jody Serey

CONTENTS

AT THE DINER IN CINCINNATI, 1975 1
AUTUMN 4
BALLET 5
BICYCLE 6
BIRD BOOK...7
BLUEBELLS 10
CARDS 11
CONFINEMENT 12
CULTURE 13
DANIEL DRIVING TO THE SEMINARY............14
DOUBTS 16
ENDINGS 17
EXPECTANT 18
FAILING 20
FIRST ADVENT 21
FOSTER CHILD 22
GIRL SCOUT COOKIES 23
GOING AFTER MISTLETOE 24
GROWING SEASON 26
HYSTERECTOMY, 1976 28
IMOGENE 29
IN THE MORNING 30
JANUARY POOL, 1974 31

JESSIE	32
JONNIE SUE	34
LANDLOCKED	45
LOVING MY ADOPTED CHILD	46
MANGER	47
MID-DAY, 1986	48
MIDNIGHT	49
MOTHER'S ATTIC	51
MY SON	53
NESTING	55
OLD WOMEN OF THE NIGHT	56
OLD WRECK	57
OUR LADY	58
PEGGY'S DOG, MISS POKEY	65
PLUM TREE	66
POTATOES	67
PRODIGAL	69
RICH GIRLS, 1970	70
RUBY	71
SISTER AMABILIS	72
STANDING IN FRONT OF ABRAHAM LINCOLN'S HAT	73
SUNDAY MORNING	74
SWEEPING GLASS	75
SWIMMING LESSON, 1957	76

THEIR WEDDING	77
TINY DEATH	78
TOTAL IMMERSION	79
TRUE LOVE, 1969	80
TRUTHS	81
VANISHED	82
VIETNAM, 1969	84
VISITING	85
WHAT REMAINS	87
WHEN I MISSED MY MOTHER	88
WHITE SHOES	89
WITH HONOR	90

AT THE DINER IN CINCINNATI, 1975

I eat my lunch with old women
to remind me who I am
under all this plumage

there are six or eight whose
faces occupy the spaces
in the little booths
but seldom more than four
smile to me when I walk in

they wear hats on their spider-web hair
and gloves on their spotted hands
purses and shopping bags burden them

they come to town to shop for
needles or for stout black shoes
and on holy days the communion rail
at the big church is lined with them,
mouths popped open
like baby birds

each one is a widow,
the half death cast back
into the dimming light and
the shadows of the children
the wedding rings twirl
where once the flesh was plump

"she is a man's" was the message
when the fingers flashed with heat
and the children stirred
in each velvet belly
like poppy seeds in the rain

"she was a man's" the thinning circles say,
still possessed by something dead
true to bones in Sunday suits

we drink tea, eat soup,
and I count out the change
for the gray-faced girl
who rattles cups
and drops the spoons

infirm magi, last Christmas
they brought their gifts to me
and among the offerings was
a handkerchief done in red,
silk thread saying "Miami Beach"

I waited for the one
who had handed me the box
to tell me why I held the bit of
cloth with a map and two words
done in stitches like a wound

my son, she said, brought this to me

she named that poppy seed,

the one who went to Florida,

the one who sent her money,

the one who died

and she had a telegram

about a soldier in Korea

I never went to Florida, but

I wept on Miami Beach

AUTUMN

the wind has brought the
leaves to cover the grass
that the man comes to mow
now that we are old

I see the things that should be done,
but I sit and watch the clouds instead
the small tasks of tidiness
come undone in hours,
but the birdsong heard, or the
lizard glimpsed along the wall
are mine to keep, as long as
I remember them

BALLET

the dance depends on friction
the rosin on the shoes,
for balance, precision, and
public elegance
art born of control,
the head held so, positioned hand,
pain all gone to power

BICYCLE

he was a parade
the glittering bike his steed,
his painted unicorn,
streamers gleaming
and the snap of flags
USA! USA! USA!

music in his head
played to his baton
and he marched beside
the magic horse
who pranced for
him alone

BIRD BOOK

I never understood the rules
at seven, in the second grade
my school got books from the government
and called them a "library"

I got a card, and a day
to wander through the stacks, a dwarf
for half an hour on Thursdays,

but they didn't say to me
"you don't have to read the book you choose"
so when I picked the one thick
with birds, I panicked

the twelve hundred pages of
nesting habits and speckled eggs
would never be read in a week
by me, who still sounded out my words.
yet, I thought I was obliged

it was spring, but no matter
the sun found me in my father's chair,
eyes stuttering through the
feathered alphabet

somewhere between partridge and pheasant
my mother sensed something more

than an ornithologist budding in me
and told me the
truth in lending

"the only thing you have to do
is pay a fine,
if you don't turn in the
book on time"

BLACK CAT

the old cat died,
and you called at night
to say at last all ties
were loosed that we had
knotted tight

eighteen years, the kitten
hunkered down into
the tattered tyrant
in your chair

the first time I heard
the way you cry
the tears were lack of sleep,
and the moth the kitten tracked
across your restless bed

I remember silence, then a
purring rumbled deep,
as four eyes watched me
cross the yard into the dark

BLUEBELLS

your ways are these:
when winter stilled the
lower fields and
the farmhouse burned
you stitched bluebells
on a blanket and
dreamed about
the child

but, he died
yet when the azure waves
swept free again
in the bottom lands
you left the new house
with your camera

your letter spilled the photograph
the meadow, or
the gleam of God
look, you wrote,
see how it is:
life returns
when robbed of death

CARDS

Christmas,
so he bought a card
"To a darling granddaughter" having spent an hour reading
verses written for
another life

he was free to wander in the store
as long as he kept moving
from rack to rack
of sentiment

his fingers caught the glitter that
rubbed off the words
Congratulations
In Deepest Sympathy
Happy Birthday
Bon Voyage
Get Well Soon

no Midas touch his, for all
he stroked turned gray
but when he wiped his nose
his nostrils sparkled gold

CONFINEMENT

he sent for her,
my grandmother,
and handed back the prize,
his wife, her child
swollen with what he'd done

faltered children, angry women
holders of ferocious hearts
stared at him to see the guilt
then focused on
the dishes in the sink

August, but I shivered
with the days that orphaned me
water woke me in the morning

CULTURE

my aunt set down the china cup to look at me:

this town is hard on certain people
I knew one lady so in love
with that piano man, that Liberace,
every Saturday she did her hair all up
and put on the tiara, the one from the parade,
and the flowered dress she had made
for her niece's wedding

she'd pull out a dining chair, one she'd needlepointed
(the stitches were so tiny
they'd nearly put her eyes out)
she'd sit there for an hour by the television
and never move, even for commercials

my aunt stood up, and went to get the kettle:

I played the violin until I caught this finger
with a corn knife – see the scar?
I took it to the bone

DANIEL DRIVING TO THE SEMINARY

the leaving was the same
as all the others
maps and coffee,
a piece of fruit,
the sandwich in the bag
to harden as the
hunger fled
the flashlight, though, was new

yesterday was gasoline and
gauges for the air
in tires measured by the one
whose name he shared:
he put a penny to the tread

"I see Lincoln's jaw," he doomed
sure that death would
stalk a way to stop
the journey to the place
that called forth
the Lazarus with thermos
and an apple

Daniel said, "Dad, it's California.
I could almost walk," but
he cried, and didn't hide
the only tears he'd sire

for sons that ended

in his only begotten one.

DOUBTS

Your eyes that pierce
the asters in September
know beauty in this, too:
a cave where bats
are twenty million
and the air from excrement
kills all others who would enter

yet forty million silent wings
fold around
the gentle beasts
hanging upside down, clinging close
together in the dark

below, the living floor retches, boils
heaves upward with the force
of insects who exist to strip
flesh from faltered,
hapless young,
those who fail the sanctuary

mighty light, please
guide my wings to rise
fly above the terror
escape me from the cruel jaws
of death that scuttles underneath
all that lives, all that waits

ENDINGS

she took the test alone
in the bathroom at her mother's
the stick said pregnant,
and pointed back at her,
an accusing finger.

so she did the right thing,
and moved in with the father
who got a job and left the music
that kept them all awake
with echoes of their own

four months gone,
she read a magazine,
in a waiting room of tired faces
and saw the ads for shoes
and shiny telephones.

two weeks later,
she sold what she could find to
sweep away the verdict
the plastic stick had held
and made her way to town,
away, away, away

EXPECTANT

August 1958,
she sat on the back steps,
cigarette smoke twisting upward in the
late summer haze.
I found her crying, and
it scared me

eight years old,
I wasn't sure what to say, so
I brought her a drink of water
with no ice because
I couldn't pull the handle on the tray
to release the cubes

she talked to me like the
adult I wasn't
"they won't listen," she said,
"they say I'm just
a nervous woman,
but something isn't right.
I should know, I'm his mother.
but that's not enough, I guess."

I sat on the step below and put my hand
on her knee while she
sipped the tap water from the
blue plastic cup.

"I'm okay, baby," she finally said
"I'm okay"

a few days later,
my father came into the bedroom
where my sister and I
were sleeping with our grandmother,
who had come to help
I saw her raise up her hand to
hold his, and I waited

his words were no surprise,
but they left my little sister curled tight,
like a nesting squirrel
"I'm so sorry, girls," he said,
"your baby brother died
I feel so bad for your poor mama"

that night, we went to visit
her summer nightgown was a
familiar pink in the hospital bed.
she held out her arms
and we leaned in softly,
as if her bones were broken
"it will be okay," she said

but it never really was

FAILING

the flesh has been a decade failing
months to years of daily loss

she watches dying with her eyes
flashing fire, sparking hope
but speaks of ending in
a voice warmed with whispers

at midnight my phone rings
to chant the litany --
children, lovers, doctors
no miracles among them

then she asks the only question:
how much have you loved me?

enough, I say.
now, too much.

FIRST ADVENT

the child turned deep
and she awoke
to listen for the women
but no fire burned,
nothing moved
and she remembered that
it was hers
to blaze and feed
in the midst of all these men

the donkey breathed, and
the husband
their burdens gone by night
she missed her mother,
the older hands, the
ones that lifted
something ancient ached

later, still later
she knew there would be noise
a din of angels,
and peasants
wild things in the cold
but now, all was silence,
all was calm
except His heartbeat,
which was her own

FOSTER CHILD

behind the door, something scrabbled
animal with forest teeth
claws for carrion
a hiss, the weasel in my trap
one paw nipped, and the rest all danced in fury
I lit a cigarette, and smoked outside the door
listening to you watch me
one eye blue against the glass
you reached your hand out
for the little ember's glow
the only flame you knew
and all you'd come to want

GIRL SCOUT COOKIES

dressed in green like a lacewing
I hauled cookies door to door;
in the rain, no salesman me
the way those cookies crumbled
unthinkable to fail, conquered by a sandwich cream
my shattered bank was ransom
I bought five boxes and fed them to the dogs

GOING AFTER MISTLETOE

Nana was there for the birth
so when her child could drive again
we went to cut the mistletoe,
grandmother and mother in the front,
babies in the back

the Dodge made its way through
dusty Arkansas, and mountain roads
powdered up in clouds
autumn deep, but the sun hadn't
given up the drought

they found the grove across a field
that reached out towards the river;
one tree held the treasure
mistletoe, green and fat with sticky pearls,
glittered towards the top

our mother handed back the keys to
a car the other couldn't drive
and slid the pen knife in her pocket
three weeks old, my sister slept as
her mother scaled the tree.

she freed the bundle from its perch,
and made a sling out of her jacket
she dropped it straight, then

found the branches down.
Nana finally asked, "and if you'd fallen?"

invaded doves sent out their call,
and I thought ghosts were waking
I cried, and hid behind the car door
our mother said to us all, "I never fall.
there's nothing here to hurt you."

GROWING SEASON

he told me, there's no garden
and I knew she was frail
phones do not yield the truth
her voice was crisp as lettuce

she claimed the rains had washed away
her plans for rows
the reds and greens lay sleeping
in packages with pictures

I recalled the Aprils
when no thunder was a threat
to her who found a universe
perfected in tomatoes

I said to him, I'll come
and I rode two thousand miles
to turn the soil for her
who had moved the earth for me

HEAT, 2018

the terrible heat set the place for him
underneath the ragged tree in back of
the old gas station
his head lay on his arms and
his eyes were closed in sleep,
practicing for death
on a splintered picnic table
in the August dust

I left some water and the twenty
I had pulled for soda
I saw his hands and knew
he'd been young a year ago

HYSTERECTOMY, 1976

mother muscle
I used to talk to you like the child
you wouldn't hold
please do it this time
but every month my supplications
fell on you, a deaf ear
in the dark
when you wept, I cradled you
one hand rocking my belly
and now your tricks
are costing us your life
I will be back
where it all began,
still childless, but no child
no dictates from the moon
and you
shall be cast away
like a stone
or something dead

IMOGENE

years after she was buried I'm not sure where,
I found an obit about her life, one that was never talked about
at the table or in lawn chairs underneath the trees

in those places, she was mentioned with eyebrows raised
until she arrived, always late, with white paper boxes filled with pickles,
or star-shaped cookies

the women said, "she spends money she doesn't have because she doesn't cook"
while I sneaked pickles, watching her earrings, or stole
a cookie with a cherry pressed deep

but in the obit with the photo and her lipsticked smile,
her years were counted as a reporter behind the lines
while others grew tomatoes
and rinsed tin foil to bring the fighting boys back home

her years when she dedicated parks in parts of town
where nobody we knew lived,
her years past 100 and she said she was glad to have lived so long,
and birthday 110 when she whispered into the reporter's microphone,
"I'm just so tired"

those years were counted when I didn't know they were hers,
because under the big tree in a lawn chair
all I heard were words from women set on what they thought they knew,
while my short legs twitched to run

IN THE MORNING

some days just break your heart
the way the light comes in
where the little boys once played
or a lily will bloom in a forgotten pot
set aside for a season, then lost
she's getting old, poor thing
you know is said
but it's not the pills
or the numbers you write down
blood pressure, glucose, heart rate
that seem so sad somehow
it's still the heart, but not the one
pushing blood into arms and legs
that want to do their work
but quit before the jobs are done

JANUARY POOL, 1974

the winter you were seeing her
I joined the Y.
swimming after work,
I treaded steam and
left the snow as
water filled my ears.

silence at the bottom,
no music reached me there.
the water in my eyes
burned away
what I'd seen at Christmas.

you laughed at my frozen suit and towel

JESSIE

she candled eggs in the basement of the house
that her son would burn down someday
but before the fire on this August morning,
humid-gray with fog from rain,
I set my bowl in the old chipped sink
to make my way to where she worked
she had invited me to watch
so after breakfast I had gone to sit
silent behind her, on a seat our ancestor
made from remnants of a tree
that grew and fell unseen,
except for the three-legged stool

Jessie, the thickened niece of Nana,
passed the eggs before the light
seeking blood clots or signs of life,
that kept them from cakes
of women wearing aprons stitched
with "Good Morning" or "Rise and Shine"
for messy jobs, Jessie kept a pillowcase
hanging on a nail

I watched Jessie pass the eggs and separate
the bad, the ones we'd eat, after we
picked out the spot, and flicked it off
she forgot I was there, so when I said,
"there's not a lot of bloods today,"

she screamed full voice, and threw an egg at me,
which hit square with her practiced aim

I ran upstairs, bare feet drumming
on the wooden steps, and hid under blankets on a
bed filled up with heat, wet and hot as a mouth
Nana came to coax me out, talking low as
voices from underneath the floor caught my name,
and finally turned it loose

Nana said, Honey, come out
she's crazy. the farm has cost her mind
come out, it's hot, that blanket's wool
come out, she won't yell at you again
come out

JONNIE SUE

I.
she is apt to say
my past remains the same
the story never changes
in the telling
she speaks the facts
and in the vapor
of a summer night
on the mountain
by the river
there is a murmur
of the truth

II.
two years old
she crouches on the bottom step
 and waits for the door to
open up above
stockinged legs walk in and out
of the room
where something dying growls
and the sound is an echo
of a voice she almost heard
but the ears too young
did not know her name
the flesh that sought
her mother out

at Christmas two winters back
and sired her who was
the final thrusting for the son
the flesh that mated with the woman
to produce an heir
and begat the solemn eyes, the girl
this flesh is falling free
of the man who wears it

III.
the wife, the mother tiptoes
from the room and closes
the door so noise will not disturb
the life that grows inside his head
so noise will not disturb
the labor of his death
she pauses in the
shadowed hall
the towels in her hand
the child looks up
the mother walks away

IV.
she walks
the smallest of the flock her hand held high
by the nearest grieving woman to the square white box
that is the church
to the square wood box
that is the father

she hears the words our father who art in heaven

and she looks at the ceiling

she looks up and expects to see him there

above them where her

sister pointed

when she asked

where he had gone

the hinges clasp

the church door shuts

other hinges do their work

all are locked away

V.

they rise above her

on their heavy legs

she darts like mercury

through the unguarded kitchen door

till one pursues who can

still run after

years of treading quietly

the child is wild

with silence

among the female forest

the sisters big as mothers

the mother small with pain

VI.

it is a womb that bed

and she waits for

the rites of passage

that will grant her

the right to sleep alone

away from the woman

who took the child

into the void

left by a man

the chasm is too great

for the little body

and so she remains

somehow, always

too small, too small

until her own womb proclaims her grown

proclaims her born

proclaims her alone

she is exiled to the guest room

with the ignoble stain

the shade of victory

VII.

the small hand wandering

found its musician's touch

and played a simple tune

on her young instrument

the melody faltered

she began again

first with low tones, then with high

until her back arched

with the song

until her heart beat
with the time
until her senses shouted to her
there it is
there it is
there it is

VIII.
that twelve-year-old she was
with the Webster's dictionary
made lists of alien words,
in English
they were a tongue apart
from the summer
that saw her bent in a
posture of faith, for
she trusted the
mystery of the letters that coiled
in and out, tendrils of a
foreign vine that climbed to
bloom at her
young window
the definitions shivered gold
the fearsome flowers of a fragrance too heady
for a child
yet she was a bride, this child,
wed to the cacophony
at so young an age
the mating caused a fever

when it found issue in
the truth that lay beside her
long before she could claim it,
lift it up for her embrace,
the mother of the pain

IX.

he hunted her
for years
the brother-in-law
seeking things in miniature
he'd married in her sister
she darted from him
quarry quickened
by the claw
that grazed her throat
and sought to tear
a flesh more tender
she fled the wing-beats
the hard black eyes
of the predator
who would lift up her sparrow bones
to maul a
season's feathers

X.

there were few ships
in West Virginia
but she had been sent

to sail on

a sea so salt

she wondered why

she had spawned the

story for the contest

that had read her words

proclaimed her wise

and exiled her, the winner

to a luxury cruise alone

she was sick at sea

not from ocean waves

but with waves of longing for the land

that she knew firm

beneath her feet

the only swell she rode with grace

waves of green alfalfa

XI.

she held her trench coat closed

an April fog

when he said

come warm me

she believed the snow

was gone

there seemed to be

a budding

please warm me

she heard the leaves

push against the

leather cages

yes warm me

she felt the grass

move far below

the pale white roots

digging darker life

come warm me

pressed

against the bloom

shoulders flat

against the weight

you warm me

all that lived was damp

XII.

they lived in little houses

moving each time

the walls closed in

moving each time

there was another door

to leave locked forever

moving each time

the view from the kitchen window

reflected back like

oil on a puddle

she held him till he

left a mark

like the wallpaper

where a picture once hung

XIII.
Christmas
she had a letter
from the tallest saying
it isn't good news
and she learned
the tiny cells growing
had built an enemy
in the one who had built daughters
exactly there
Easter
brought the ice to her
and the others
huddled once again
against the dark while she suffered
grew cold
then felt no more

XIV.
a spring
a single burst of lilacs
the breath of purple
in shades of night
would become to her like
deadly nightshade
she would later
breathe the heavy
burden of the bush
and remember how the scent of blossoms

how the scent of woman
married in that room
to leave her breathless

XV.
she left
she went to
flood her heart
with a desert
she went to Arizona
and waited for
a sun a fire
a flame
hot enough to
burn away
all of
West Virginia

KITCHEN DANCE, 1986

my young sons
share the radio
they find a rhythm
seek a beat
and find in me
their partner

today I hold them
without heat
as we turn by the stove
but I know
someday those they lie with,
or to,
will blame me for
the excess

they will say:
"your mother's skeletons
are lodging in your bones"

but today we dance
to music someone's playing

LANDLOCKED

I look at photos of old houses in Maine,
but I've breathed the desert air too long

I will never leave

Some years the rain just sets the sun aside
and other summers send the floods that
drown both heat and horses
there is nowhere for me to go where memories
of faded sons and favorite dogs
won't find me in the mornings
when the hummingbirds chitter and
buzz the feeders
I have scattered sacred dust among the grit
of granite hills and red rock cliffs
Christian names and those on collars are honored
from my porch among the thorns and flowers

I will never leave

LOVING MY ADOPTED CHILD

I loved her in that breathless gasp
of the old mother who felt the stir
she was the child who changed
the crone to champion
no madonna, for one fist held
the sword as one hand
held her own
I could have killed what would
cause her tears

now we have aged,
her beauty marked by
what I never was
and me by years bringing
what I could not
we feed the birds and share our words
in ordinary ways
she does not know that covered deep
is the glitter of my blade

MANGER

there was a desert then
trod upon by kings and camels
who sought the star-lit child

no snow, but a cold that crept
and made the mother rise
to take the blanket
from her arms and
wrap it around the boy

baby unaware, how could you know
the sound of angels,
the journey of the men?

yet, I am sure you
felt the wind, then heard
the heartbeat of the woman
who came to hold you close

MID-DAY, 1986

my babies found the shade
with the Indian women who
took them while I worked
through the wavering window
I glanced up to see them play,
their clothes hung up for later
flashing like sunfish,
they darted into view
from under trees as black as water

MIDNIGHT

like the snake goes back
to quail's eggs
you returned and
caught me
sleeping

the bed was mine, and
the solitude.
their price was met
in full

the dog thought you
were home
and her tail skipped twice
and then my heart
how cruel to hear
your keys drop on the dresser

darkness, yet I knew the weight
and heard the voice like dreaming
then dreaming fell,
then the sheets

MIXED MARRIAGE, 1990

in Big Stone at the café
she had made him breakfast
her eyes too tired for ten o'clock
it took him days to mention college
or the tennis racket in his car
she had touched his sleeping bag
with fingers asking questions
but made no comment on his boots that
waited, empty, like locust shells

they bought the license in the spring,
then stopped to tell her mother
his parents sent a check, which he
drove a hundred miles to cash,
and copies of prescriptions

he learned to drop his eyes, and
fish in silence on the river
his adjusted grip could field-gut rabbits
or wrap around the ax
her brothers claimed him when the evenings
echoed crickets, and the moon was blue
she'd see him disappear
with the bottle and the men

MOTHER'S ATTIC

Mother's attic
it's all there
wrapped in cotton like a wound

sometimes, furtive as a thief,
I rummage through her chest
it's all laid bare

the rattle with my teethmarks
a little knitted cap
a ribbon and photographs
taken with Santa Claus
and a husband
amputated curls
letters home
the quilt begun for my dead son

I half expect my lovers to be there
swathed in paper with my dolls
face paint peeling in the dark
shoes tied on with string

MOTHERS DAY, 1958

she waited until May to wear her pride
the linen suit with the pleats that fanned against the prize,
the late-life child, the one to change the world

the daughters had given her the candy before church;
the flowers that she wore were pink, because
her mother was alive

the scent of starch, and the perfume
he'd bought at Christmas, the kind she'd
worn when they were young

her alto pushed against the notes
of hymns she sang without the book,
her voice bright with certainty

in September driving home
from the little cemetery, she said
I was a fool to be so happy

MY SON

my son,
you won't be borne
when my body
welcomed you
and your
faceless father
there were those who
shouted wait!
the growing season is forever
to one so young
I waited out my spring little boy
then summer bore a
sun too hot
for this field
all life seared
and I shone clean
as if sown with salt
I'm sewn with thread

baby, baby
ghost child

I would have haunted you
with these arms
muscles made taut
reaching up
for things
handed down
to other women

NEIGHBORS, 1988

home now in the daylight,
I meet the women
who watch their husbands
flee the suburbs in the morning

they appear for the school bus,
dragging children like Christmas dolls
and send them two by two
into the yellow ark

they eye me with distrust,
the one who writes
and waits for the mailman,
my god's messenger

one woman, her arms full of yorkies,
and coffee in her voice
did speak to me at noon
as I searched the box for hope

"anything today?"

NESTING

storks feed their old ones
the ragged birds,
the ones whose flight
folds stiff
against their sides

eyes glint bright,
and see the sea
where younger beaks
dip down to catch
what will feed
downy young, tattered old

they all wait as nestlings
listening for wing-beats

OLD WOMEN OF THE NIGHT

the old women of the night
wash their stockings by starlight
dipping down into the water
to come up streaming
you can hear them at the river
when the village lies asleep
creeping down to the banks
as furtive as weasels
to pull their sour skirts around their waists
and strip the dusty tatters down
toes like rows of saw teeth
they lean their frowzy head together
to trade the tales of birth pangs,
wild roots, and the moon
faces dead a thousand times
limp as tea leaves in their minds
scant death beds now those bosoms
that rocked away the fires of
a score of summers, a throng of Augusts
breasts as flat as stepping stones
worn away by ripples
of the mouths who came
to seek them, hungry all,
the lovers and the children
drinking down the flow
using up the life

OLD WRECK

you said the Ford was the
last car you'd ever buy
and set out to keep your word

the touch-up paint kept
all the marks
from showing

tires and oil, and a
buffing cloth
helped deny the miles

but inside where it counted
your road was long,
and when you died
the car said fifteen oh-oh-oh

original? I was asked
when I took it in for service
one of a kind, I said

OUR LADY

they all came to stare,
the pirates and the pilgrims,
rape and relics in their midst,
wearing amulets

some pried at the little
jewel that wouldn't yield,
wielding supplications like knife blades
working up great beads of sweat
in lust
or adoration

yet it sat, tight in the navel of
our lady

they scarcely glanced at her pearly breasts,
two shells cast up from sorrow
the sour sea
had left a dowry
but no one claimed the bride,
great with child,
and salt

in the wound it had grown, the child,
fins rippling in the waves
the beauty of its scales
yet to be revealed,

yes it swam,
and with grace
it moved
blessed was the fruit of her wound

she'd brought it forth, and touched
its lidless eyes with joy for
it saw everything

the silver gills moving found
nothing in her arms
to breathe
so she placed her bounty in the water,
our lady of the ebb tide
and saw the spear leave the
hidden hand
heard the cry
that danced in the mist for days

she paced the shore and felt
the empty place where
the child had fed
and knew she would be barren
except to those who would carve
her name in plaster

she fell upon the shore until
the shellfish felt her shame
and covered her until

she lay, a white rigid pearl,
in the hollow that had been her belly,
a sand crab placed a jewel,
ripped from the crown of
a king he'd watched drown

the gulls clacked their beaks
and screamed their joy
until those
who dwelled
among the dunes
came down to hunt the sound

OUT OF BODY EXPERIENCE

out of body experience
that broken toy,
would you have me claim it?
it was no prize with
all its pieces

besides,

the view from the ceiling
is my reward for the
final forgetting

and that white light is an angel
not some neon mirage
as you would claim
if you saw it

Christ, what a glow

I call it finished
I never really began it
and the false starts weren't worth the dust

you'd coax me back to a
rag doll, its stuffing
gone to mice

standing by that bed, you tell jokes
to that dead-faced mirror of me
chanting litanies of punchlines

I perch here on this fixture

and dangle my chiffon legs
they float, and you look
right through them

your breath moves me to
drift towards your hand
to see if we still touch, I
reach for you

you still can't grasp
the stuff I'm made of

OUT OF PRINT

after a century,
it was mine

the book called *The Young Wife's Help*
gave recipes for johnny cake
cures for garden blight
dates for butchering
remedies for colic
advice on modesty and voice
and hints for dying on the farm

my apple pie was adequate, but
my training lacked in
making up the
proper death bed
luckily, there was a chart

had she known, my grandmother?
the coverings to save the mattress,
layers to spare the down
the words "soiling of the linens after
the beloved has expired"
told me more of fate than Sartre

my grandmother,
a festival of regulations
and the last of hers to live

why didn't she say
"you wet your pants when you die"?

I would have been so careful
in the car and
in the city
and the chances taken would
have been free of strangers

had she watched me,
arrogant in the plum tree,
and remembered moving into rooms
busied with blankets
speaking low,
saying words to send
the boys to draw the
water for the washing?

PEGGY'S DOG, MISS POKEY

if the last is first,
and peacemakers are blessed,
then your place is at the foot
of whatever angel meets us all
when we climb the stairs to
where you'll be.

cherubims aside,
there is no heaven without friends
whose four legs have walked
the rocky roads
that we have known and
stumbled on.

let the saints
do their work
as well as you did yours

PLUM TREE

the old plum tree was never safe,
brittle, and always dying,
twisted dark like winter
the spring days I felt alive

she said don't climb it, it's weak
yet she braced the branch
that still bore fruit,
and kept the bird house there

she told me this tree's an old woman
worn out from working,
and fighting back the wind
there's nothing here to save it

I watched the plums grow fat,
and kept the birds away.
I waved my arms and
set loose a leaf that lingered

POTATOES

Arizona summer
but the pots and little beds,
still bulged with what she did

one time,
white lilacs that
don't grow here,
but there they were,
in a bucket filled with dirt

as I marveled,
she said, "sorry they're not purple.
but they still smell."
my face was breathing flowers,
so I couldn't answer

another time,
she ordered from
a catalog to grow potatoes
a sort of canvas barrel
with windows on two sides
that opened up to show
what was growing out of sight

she later called and said,
"I want to show you something"
so I went to see.

but first, the Pepsi sacrament
in plastic cups with ice,
beneath a ragged tree

we talked, and sorted through
the sacred and profane
of our intersected days
and then, and only then,
we turned to face the barrel

with the angled wrist of a
flamenco dancer,
she unzipped one side, and
folded down the flap

the hatchlings nestled there,
held by dirt, and safe from all
but Peggy

"see?" she said, "potatoes, potatoes in a barrel."
I touched their baby skin, and
then returned them to the dark
one quick zip, and they were gone again

PRODIGAL

when travels meant a trunk covered
with stickers of the cities
the journey was in proportion
to the labels of the past

the miles all lay behind and
nothing gave a clue as
to what map would measure out
the miles that owned the road

today it's backpacks and photos
taken with your phone, and I see
bits of what you let go by as you
walk away from home

your tattoos, which vine
around your arms
tell me what you never say

RICH GIRLS, 1970

the rich girls hung together,
gold and cashmere sweaters,
their purses double of my rent,
and filled with cards
that took them
where I'd never go

I stepped around them on my
way to class, or the place that I
sometimes worked so I could buy
the good shampoo, or oil for
the car I seldom drove
to save the gas

RUBY

raiding Tennessee,
he took her west
away from the hills
and her pale family
her slow look and
simple hands
were foreigners
for the women
in his clan
the mother and the sisters
at the airport
met his mountain bride
like tourists

he bought chairs and
dishes for his house
and watched in silence
when she cooked
the little knife
she'd brought from home
turning in her palm

SISTER AMABILIS

that February at school,
she heard her lover's voice,
dreams darkened with his call
she sold her books and
sent her cat home
to her sister

the convent door slammed shut
as she faced the other women
the rustle of His brides
the whisper of their shoes
like prayers, or the
wind outside her window

the laundry room her chapel
the wetness and the heat
as she did the work to
earn His glance
His shroud mixed in
with sheets

STANDING IN FRONT OF ABRAHAM LINCOLN'S HAT

it waited behind bullet-proof glass,
and the irony of that was the only thing
that made me smile
that winter day at the museum.
I passed by Mary's silver set,
and books that would not be read again
to the hat, the hat, the hat!
the ordinary wear hat, not the one for
portraits or the theater, and
that April night

its worn spots were from him,
his hands, the bald spot on the brim
where he touched to be polite,
or from weather where
he walked against the wind
with thoughts that history claims to know,
but must have been only his,
in a crowd, or alone at night
as others slept and left him
awake to save the country

SUNDAY MORNING

your sideways face
slept unaware
I'd been awake for hours
wondering where my shoes
had gone
my eyes took in the room
and you breathed on

I thought I saw my coat

the sound of rain and
the ones whose house this was
making tea and toast
I heard the kettle
bang the sink
I longed to be
so plain

SWEEPING GLASS

my mother's way of
sweeping glass
is the one I use

whatever has shattered
I ease towards the brown bag
carefully, carefully I tease shards
until they disappear into my paper safety

I hunt the danger down
and check for stragglers
lurking
to bleed me later
whatever has been shattered

SWIMMING LESSON, 1957

I was tall for seven,
and too polite to say
I was in the wrong class
at the public pool
so when they said go off the board
I went and hoped they'd know
I couldn't be there long

I drifted on the bottom of the pool, and
watched the bubbles come
from a square hole in the side
the tiles were blue, and later I heard
the crewcut with the whistle say,
she's supposed to be a tadpole
and you put her with the guppies

THEIR WEDDING

as this new love makes one of two

an old love knows her child

my smile goes forward, yet

my heart looks backward

where you were

a step ago

a heartbeat

a breath

TINY DEATH

such a simple sleep, little brother
the last fifty years I wondered who
you would have been
had September not brought
your birth and death
together

curled in your little box,
quiet as the seasons send down
the rain down the snow
down the roots of
the tree that wrap around
your heart

you are safe in the realm of
what might have been and mourned
for what you never were
your decay private and
confined to the four walls of
 your world

a clean slate, little brother
you are flawless in your nightgown
your ashes fine as flour
your tiny imperfections
gently sifted clean while
you sleep

TOTAL IMMERSION

you made me dishcloths
edged in stitches
fine enough for brides
I never felt right about
washing off the breakfast eggs

yet I did because I knew
you'd think I didn't love
your gift,
or somehow you

TRUE LOVE, 1969

thinking back, I realized he'd
rolled out of bed with her and mailed
his high school ring to me

I had wanted it for years,
but now in the Friday mail
at the college where I
waited to be free
of books and expectations
I no longer felt the touch
of anything but gold
and a big blue stone

I wonder now if the she
in long years of shes
asked where he was going
I could almost hear his voice say,
there's something I need to do,
I won't be long

eventually, the diamond ring
came from a commissary overseas
I let it sit all day with a note from home
my mother wrote while waiting
for her hair to dry

TRUTHS

kitchen tables and campfires,
wherever the circle collects
are cathedrals of worship
for legends of what is
known to those
who hold the truth
in coffee cups
and trembling hands

VANISHED

his hands are what I know
pocked from months in a plastic box
two years before I
felt his grip as he looked at me

he had no chance of life, they said
when he arrived in the ER
dangling from the other mother
with his dying twin

I saw their photo once, before the
social worker's folder shut
they looked like baby birds
plucked from the sidewalk
after wind, or a cat,
yet he had lived, but was alone

his surgeries filled cabinets with
papers I could never see,
the adoption was closed,
but my heart was told
to open wide for the boy

his baby heart had stopped
and his chest showed wounds
of what had healed, but what had not
lay deep and waiting in the dark
I dream of his old man's hands

the tiny boy was
clover beneath the stone
that makes it to the sunlight
yet never blooms green,
but the bees come anyway

somehow he grew, but
the man could not sustain
what the scars had tried to knit
his sleep ended dreams, and
sent strangers to my gate

VIETNAM, 1969

he got busted in Vietnam
not for junk like some
of his buddies but for handing out rubbers
to the men in
the village
it was theft of government property and
a C.O. who had it
for his ass
and trailed him
like he was
a bitch in heat so, when the boxes disappeared,
the ones designated
to protect Our Boys Abroad
from the broads abroad,
when they disappeared because he thought it would be better
to have fewer babies
to blow up
and a little less clap
when those boxes disappeared,
they got him

VISITING

in 1956
with rolls of paper
and wax crayons
we visited the graves
of those in tintypes
and the lockets
family cemetery

I was mesmerized
by the hunt
part picnic, part archeology,
and touch of
Baptist witchcraft
epitaphs and old disease
prairie incantations
I could barely read
what came alive
in rubbing

my job was coloring, going
straight in one direction
crayon firm and stroking
fading words to view:
"Beloved Wife and Tender Mother"
"Our Angel Is His Angel Now"
"Not Gone Is He, But Just Away"
 the dead ones all were poets

I ate the sandwich, peeled the egg
and hid the apple cores
among the peonies in jars
of dusty hollyhocks
while thickened aunts and my
young mother
strolled among the stones
papers crackling in the breeze
of Indiana's June
they pulled weeds, pushed back the grass
and hovered low like bees
made slow by heat
and heaviness of
endless summer flowers

WHAT REMAINS

this box
the dust of my boy
should be like frankincense or
whatever else the Three Kings
packed to travel
instead,
black plastic and a bar code
adorn the little shipping coffin
of my son, my child, my heart

I signed the delivery slip
the mail carrier held
grateful for a small task
that still said you're mine
even though the galaxies
slide past as you fly free
while we, ever older,
stagger to stand down here
below

WHEN I MISSED MY MOTHER

when I missed my mother I'd go
buy coffee from the woman who
called me "honey"
and asked me how my day had been

I'd sit on the cracked plastic seat
at the counter like
some adult elf
on a giant metal toadstool

the coffee was always bitter and
she never remembered my spoon
but she smiled
whenever I needed her

WHITE SHOES

my mother caught me at the sink and
whispered in my ear,
he's put out white shoes for your wedding day
I rubbed the dish and whispered back,
it's a backyard wedding, so who cares?

and she said, I guess you're right,
but the 70s are over
just barely, I replied, and he's
still so happy with those shoes,
and he bought the belt to match

don't hurt his pride, I said to her,
he'll think I made you do it
she nodded twice, and in
the pictures from that afternoon
we all are smiling

WITH HONOR

no comfort knowing
that I am not the first,
nor millionth from the last,
just one beneath the cross,
as the son bled god
the mother, dreamless now,
flickering, a shadow
of a moth
around an ancient fire

aren't you proud? and I say
I am frozen.
rigid with worship
I have touched his uniform,
robe of a holy man,
yet beneath the cloth
I feel the boy
and know his face
in clouded light,
breathing sleep into the dark

Printed in the USA
CPSIA information can be obtained
at www.ICGtesting.com
JSHW080912181124
73796JS00003B/15

9 781881 276340